SIMPLE FISHING WITH BREAD

The Secret?
Experience!

Lelio Zeloni

Copyright © 2018 Lelio Zeloni

All rights reserved

ISBN: 978-1-80111-643-5

First English Edition: March 2019
Original edition: December 2018 "La Pesca Semplice con il Pane - Il Vero Segreto? L'Esperienza!"

Author:

Lelio Zeloni was born in Prato on August 8th, 1953. Since he was an adolescent, he has had two passions, painting and fishing. Over the years he has practiced spinning, fly fishing, tenkara and of course his favourite, fishing with bread. These experiences with different techniques, have helped him to become the expert fisherman that he is today.

Reproductions made for professional, economic or commercial purposes or for uses other than personal use can only be made following specific authorization issued by the author.

CONTENTS

	PREFACE	5
	INTRODUCTION	9
1.	THE BEGINNING	11
2.	THE FLOATS	29
3.	THE RIGHT ATTITUDE FOR FISHING	35
4.	THE RIGHT TECHNIQUE	41
5.	WHICH TYPE OF BREAD ARE BEST FOR FISHING	47
6.	LET'S AVOID UNNECESSARY EQUIPMENT	53
7.	IMPORTANT THINGS TO KNOW	63
8.	MINIMUM FISH MEASUREMENTS	65
9.	THE TYPE OF FISH YOU CAN CATCH WITH BREAD	69
	CONCLUSION	99

Preface

At the end of the nineteenth century, the economist Vilfredo Pareto discovered that 80% of the world's wealth and income was produced by 20% of the population. You are probably now wondering, "What does this have to do with a book about fishing?" A lot!

Let me tell you about the Principle of Pareto, also known as the 80/20 Law. The principle states that about 20% of causes create 80% of effects. So, 80% of what we get is caused by only 20% of what we do.

In every field or sector, most of the effects are caused by a limited number of causes.

So, you will notice with great surprise that 80% of the world's wealth is held by 20% of the population, 80% of a company's earnings are generated by 20% of the sales, 80% of your results are generated by 20% of your actions.

This principle is present in many areas of our life.

Even fishing is not immune to this principle. Remember, 20% of what you do generates 80% of your results.

So, if most of the results come from a small part of our actions, it means that most of what we do is of little value and is quite useless.

This book perfectly embodies the principle of Pareto. These pages, that are written in a very simple way, are very effective, they are the essence of experience that will teach you that 20% will give you 80% of the value, leaving out all that is irrelevant and unnecessary for successful fishing.

Do you want to know something? It is the first time I have written the preface of a book and I am writing it for my father's book.

I must confess, I was a bit moved when I read this book. While reading it, many memories came to mind. During adolescence I often went fishing with my father and my friends, especially in the summer.

Our favourite destination was the Seggio river at Marina di Castagneto Carducci. I remember the enjoyment of being in company and appreciating simplicity, if I close my eyes and think about it, I can hear my friends' laughter in the distance and the sound of the sea breeze that caresses the river reeds.

My father has always taught me to respect nature, the environment and animals. This is also why we always threw the fish back into the water, but above all, we always left the fishing spot clean.

When you go fishing, dear readers, please remember to protect the environment.

But you have bought this book because you want to improve your fishing, so happy reading.

Dr. Edoardo Zeloni Magelli

Introduction

This easy to learn book wants to be a useful guide both for those who want to start fishing with bread, and for the more experienced fishermen who want to improve their fishing skills.

In these pages you will find very practical tips on how to fish with bread, you will have a picture of the ideal bread varieties, you will learn how to prepare your bait and put it on the fishhook properly.

Bread is a philosophical bait, it's suitable for many fish and thanks to its aroma once in the water, it releases a very enticing trail, attracting many schools of fish within the fishing rod's range.

The scent is so attracting to them that often the fish do not even notice whether the fishing line is done up well or not, this is why it is always a good idea to have some nylon and a bigger fishhook that can avoid us surprises in case we catch a bigger fish.

Of course, I will not only speak about bread, you will

find advice on the various types of floats and the best ones to use, both in calm and rough seas, and on the length of the rods to use which will depend on where we choose to go fishing.

I will teach you how to recognize the suitable places for fishing, teaching you how to use your logic, but above all, you will understand when it is time to go fishing by observing the tides.

Over time you will acquire the sense of water, which will also help you understand where to find the fish and therefore catch them, giving you great satisfaction.

From an editorial point of view, it will surely not be perfect, so I hope you will forgive me, what matters is that you learn to fish.

I also took pleasure in drawing the illustrations of this book myself, drawing and painting have always been (together with fishing) my great passions, but this is another story.

A special thanks for the creation of this book, goes to my son Edoardo, I must also thank my wife Donatella for the photographs and my daughter Carlotta, for the graphics and video. Thank you so much.

Happy reading.

1. THE BEGINNING

My dear fishermen friends, if I was told, when I was a boy, that one day I would write a book about fishing, I would never have believed it, but it really happened.

When we reach a certain age, we feel the need to leave traces of our time on earth, we feel the desire to transmit our experience into something where we perform well.

I have dedicated a whole lifetime to fishing, experimenting many techniques. I practiced spinning, fly fishing, Tenkara and of course my favourite, fishing with bread. These different techniques have developed in me what I call "the sense of water".

In any fishing spot I go, I understand where the fish are and approach them in the right way by using simple logic.

If you follow my simple but effective advice, you will also develop this sense in a short time and you will become excellent fishermen.

In the short time you dedicate to reading this book, I will transmit all my experience of fishing to you. Think of how lucky you are, I have spent a lifetime learning what I know, while you will have learnt it in a few hours.

A big secret is experience, that has been lived and full of many mistakes, doubts (very many) but that was necessary to for me to me become the fisherman I am.

There are two types of fishermen, one catches the water while the other catches the fish.

I was the one who caught water, I never caught anything but I watched those with admiration who, next to me, caught many fish. I used to say:

"They catch fish because they are lucky"

Wrong! They catch fish because they fish in the right way.

They had a good fishing rod, a good reel, a perfect line and the right bait, but above all, they knew the technique well.

All things I did not have.

I kept watching these fishermen, I studied them, always trying to learn something, sometimes I also asked them for advice, but they were not always willing to give it to me.

Maybe because I was just a boy and they did not want to waste time with me, I was the fisherman of many failures, with a lot of wrong equipment and who never managed to catch a fish.

However, mistakes are a great source of learning.

One of the first things I understood, which is also the most important thing when fishing at sea, is to learn to observe the tides. It is useless to fish when the sea withdraws, the fish go out at sea (low tide). It is correct to fish when the tide comes back bringing the fish with it (high tide).

Another doubt I always had was regarding the bait. I always listened to the fishermen talking to each other, some used earthworms, others used koreans, some shrimps, and others artificial baits and bread etc...

What a mess!

Of course, each type of fish requires its own bait if we want to catch it.

I was a very shy boy and I found it difficult to go to the hunting and fishing shop, because I didn't know which type of bait to buy.

It was 1967, I was 14 years old and I was in Castiglioncello, where every August me and my whole family spent our holidays.

My parents had given me a fishing rod, the classic "Fiorentina". It was a grafted rod, made of a material that was called "sweet cane", it was made of 4 pieces, each one was 1.50 meters long for a total of 6 meters.

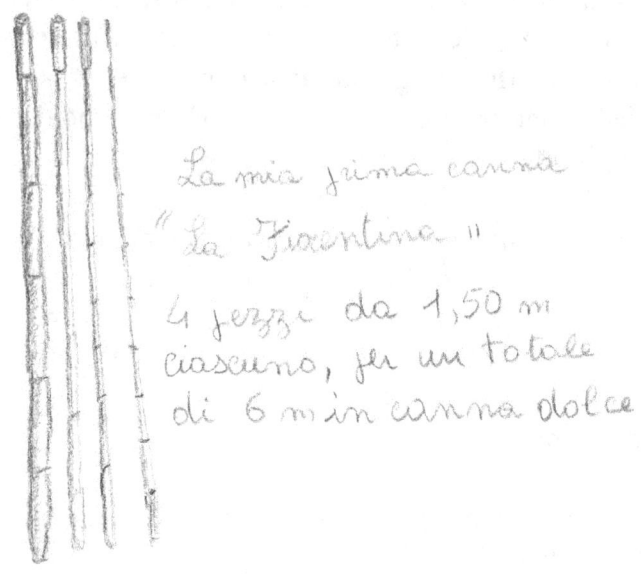

Fig. 1: *My first "Fiorentina" fishing rod*

4 pieces, 1,50 mt each, for a total of 6 mt of "sweet cane"

I began to fish both in the river and in the sea with that rod. But inside me, was the usual doubt. What bait should I use?

One day, while observing some fishermen on the rocks when I was at Bagno Tre Scogli in Castiglioncello, I noticed that they had a small bucket next to them into which they placed pieces of bread.

They took these pieces of bread, soaked them in water and then squeezed them with their hands, then they put the bread in a cotton rag, holding it in their left hand pulling the rag up on all four sides, and with their right hand they turned the ball of bread that was inside the rag squeezing it as much as possible, like when you wring a leather cloth to dry your car.

These images remained impressed in my mind, in fact, driven by curiosity, I decided, to try it as well.

Maybe I would finally resolve my doubt on the bait to use.

I had bread at home, and I thought it was bait that I would have available at all times.

Fantastic, I thought full of enthusiasm, I took a few slices of bread, I soaked them in water, I squeezed them as I had observed and went on the rocks to try to fish.

I put the fishing rod together, the line was the same as the one I used to fish in the river. I do not remember what type of line and hook I used to fish, I only remember that I had a very common float that was not very appropriate. That's all I had available.

So far so good, the best came later. I put the bread on the hook and did several throws, but the bread always fell off, it came off the hook and fell into the water. If there was a positive thing I had though, it was perseverance.

Someone who was watching me, perhaps moved by pity, pointed out to me that the bread was still very wet, so he helped me prepare the bait. He took a small ball of bread, put it on the hook and began to work it thoroughly, he turned it, and continued to turn it until it was the shape of a small pear.

"Try now!" He said.

Wonderful!

I managed to launch without losing the bread, I watched the float with excitement, then I saw it sink and the gentleman said:

"Pull!"

I must have pulled late because I didn't catch anything. This gentleman said:

"Try again, when you see the float move, pull immediately, bread is not like an earthworm, it immediately comes off the hook"

I tried again, excited by the fact I was being observed, I paid more attention. As soon as I saw the float move, I pulled, not in a convinced way, but when I felt a slight pull and saw a silver reflection moving in the water, I realized that finally, this time, I had caught a fish.

"I got it, I got it I got it!"

I shouted several times, I had the glowing expression of someone who had finally reached his goal. My first fish caught at sea, just think, what a joy!

I looked at the faces of the people who were there and I saw that they were looking at me in a pleased way and they were laughing.

They understood my joy. It was my first time, my first fish!

This kind of emotion can never be forgotten, it's an emotion that lasts in the mind forever, it cannot be erased, it is permanent, it shapes the individual psyche.

Very often, even today, I get emotional when I'm fishing on the rocks and I see some young boys with their expressions of joy next to me when they catch a fish.

That moment, those young boys, the joy catching a fish, takes me back to my same past moment, and a phrase that I read in a book by Marcel Proust "Swann's Way" comes to mind.

"Will that memory ever touch the surface of my full consciousness, the ancient moment that the attraction of an identical moment has come so far to recall, to move and lift in the depths of myself? I do not know"

Year after year I became more and more experienced, I began to catch different types of fish, sea breams, goldlines, bogues, mullets, the small ones though.

I realized that I could catch different kinds of fish with bread. Perfect I thought, it's the perfect bait for me.

From my summers in Castoglioncello to now I have always gone fishing with bread.

After getting married and after the birth of my son Edoardo (1984), my wife and I decided to start camping, I felt the need to lose myself in nature.

We chose a very different campsite compared to others, in Tuscany, in Marina di Castagneto Carducci, near Donoratico on the coast of Livorno. It was a place where you could breathe true nature, we could say that it was a forest behind the sea dunes.

It was perfect because it gave me the opportunity to fish in the sea and in the river as there was a river nearby called "Il Canale" (The Canal), and the river "Seggio".

You can't imagine how many times I fished both in the sea and in the canal. In this river there were many mullets, some of them where big ones.

The banks and the ocean floors were full of earthworms.

I remember that before fishing we would take a shovel and dig up the mire from the ocean floor, we would put it on the shore next to us, then the water would drain away from the mud mixed with sand and the worms would come out.

It was a great experience to find bait on the spot, this made us feel like real fishermen.

However, after a few times, I went back to fishing with bread, because it is a much simpler and cleaner type of fishing.

The water in the canal was still and opaque and the fishing technique I used was this:

- The most sensitive float possible

- 0.18 thread

- hook n 10 covered with a small pear-shaped ball of dough

- We fished close to the bottom

Of course, the place was baited with bread, in that way we were on the safe side. We fished both in the early morning and in the afternoon.

There were so many mullets and they took the bait at all times. We used to throw them back in because the water was not the best quality, we only had fun catching them.

After 20 years spent in Marina di Castagneto, and having fished in the sea and in the river and having tried different types of baits techniques, I can tell you that the best bait is bread.

After many years of vacation in Marina di Castagneto Carducci, we decided to try Vada, also on the coast of Livorno in Tuscany, there was also a forest behind the sea dunes and of course, some excellent places to fish.

There were small cliffs on the sea, some were artificial reefs, others were simple breakwaters, while others bordered some seaside resorts.

They surely were some excellent places to fish, in fact it was full of fishermen in the morning. I wanted to discover the new place with the eye of a fisherman, and I began to examine the area to get to know it better.

I started to watch fishing, but with great disappointment I didn't see anyone catch anything.

I immediately understood why, the sea had withdrawn, the rocks that had remained uncovered were still wet, and of course, when the sea withdraws it takes everything that the fish eat with it, and as a consequence, even the fish, at that moment are out at sea.

This movement of the sea is called the low tide.

Fishing is not advisable with this type of tide, it is a waste of time because only small fish remain that hardly bite.

The right time to fish is when the tide is high, you will notice that slowly the water will cover the rocks that were left uncovered and on this occasion all the fish that had gone away will come back.

You have to bait the place with handfuls of wet and crumbed bread at regular intervals so that the fish stay there.

The more the bread flakes apart and floats the more the fish will remain in the area.

You will see lots of movement in the water, it will be a continuous rush of greedy fish.

You will see the bigger fish squashing the smaller ones. Mullets will be the first to arrive then the sea beams, leerfish, etc…

These are the classic surface fish.

If you also throw some compact dough the size of a lemon, this will quickly fall to the bottom attracting sea breams, gold lines, gilthead breams and all those fish that live on the bottom of the sea.

Imagine yourself on the fishing spot. You have understood that is the right moment to fish, the tide is high, you have been baiting and the bread is beginning to work. Now you just have to prepare your fishing rod.

You can fish with a fixed rod or with what we call a "bolognese" rod.

Fig. 2: *Fixed telescopic rod, all the pieces are inside.*

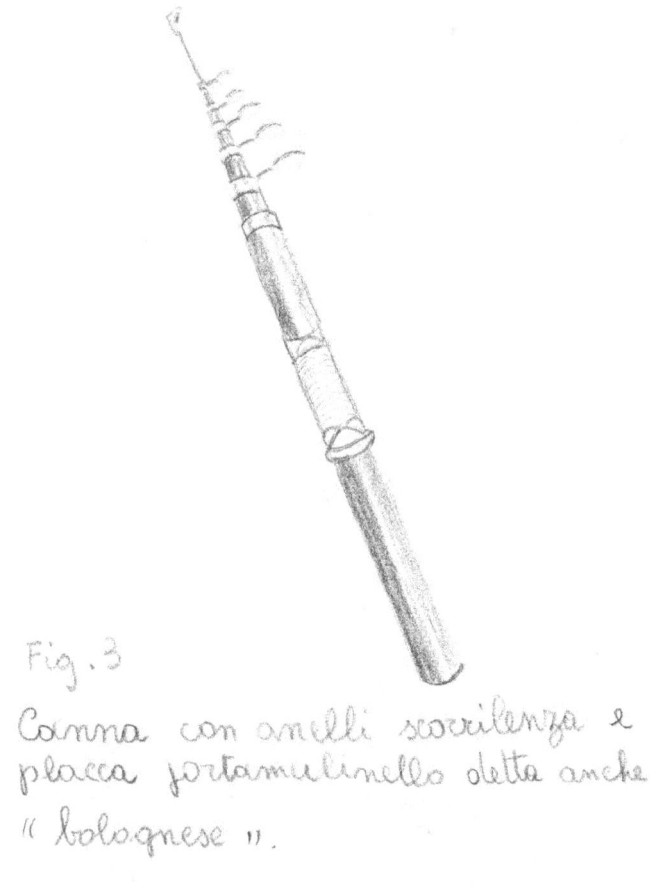

Fig. 3
Canna con anelli scorrilenza e placca portamulinello detta anche « bolognese ».

Fig. 3: *Rod with rings for the sliding fishing line and a reel holder plate also called "Bolognese".*

The fisherman who starts fishing with a fixed rod will always carry a greater amount of experience compared to a one who has not tried this technique.

When he catches a quality fish, it will only be his experience and his knowledge of the use of his rod that allows him to bring it to shore.

It is much easier to prepare the fishing line with a lighter lead weight, because, in this case you fish closer to the shore and therefore you see the fish biting better.

Fixed rods vary in length from 4.50mt to 6.50 mt long. In some cases, like fishing on the high cliffs, 7 me rods are also good.

But the classic "Bolognese" rod is also very useful, it gives us extra safety when pulling back and thanks to the friction of the reel we can use thinner ends and of course have the possibility to fish further from the shore.

2. FLOATS

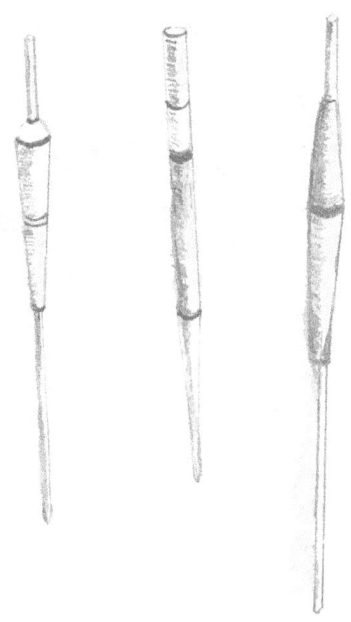

Galleggianti a forma affusolata consigliati per acque calme.

Tapered shaped floats recommended for calm waters.

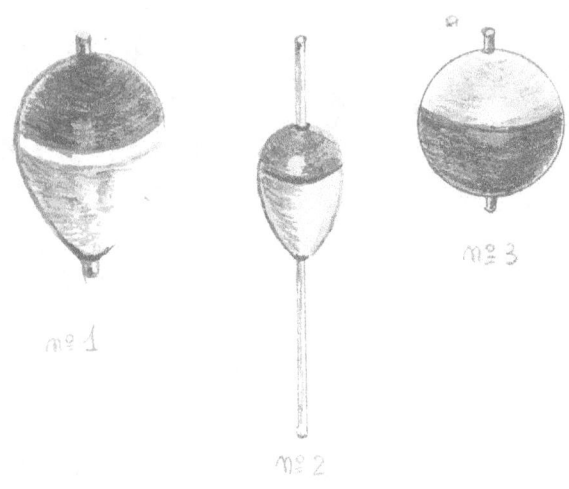

n°1 e n°2 galleggianti a fera fer acque semicalme

n°3 modello sferico fer acque mosse

n°1 e n°2: *Pear shaped floats for semi-calm waters*
n°3: *The round shape model for rough waters*

How to choose the right float? It's easy. Observe the surface of the water, you will understand if it is calm, slightly wavy or very rough. This will help you choose the float.

This is the rule: the calmer the waters are, the more sensitive the float must be, so one with a thin and long shape is good.

Color and shape are not important.

There are many floats on the market and they all work, what is important for you is visibility.

The right float for you is the one that best shows you the fish biting.

When the water is calm and I want to fish a little further out, by that I mean further from the shore, with great pleasure I use the English float, from the 4 + 1 to the 6 + 2.

These numbers are written on the bottom of the float, +1 or +2 means that we can still add 1 or 2 grams of lead if we want to.

This allows you to get the float further away and also to increase its sensitivity, thanks to this, you will be able to see the fish biting very well.

When the water becomes rougher, you should use the egg-shaped or ball-shaped floats. The more rounded the shape is, the better it will float.

You can choose the ones that are already loaded with sinkers. They are excellent for surface fishing, for mullets, saddled breams, bogues etc...

Personally, I prefer the ones that are already equipt with sinkers from 2 to 20 gms. If the fish are close to the reef, I recommend light sinkers, but if the fish are further away, I recommend the heavier ones.

At this point I think you're wondering what nylon thread to use. This will depend on the type of fish you want to catch.

If there aren't any salps, you can fish with a 0.12 or 0.14 end. If there are salps then it's better to go up to 0.20 and now, I'll immediately explain why.

When I used to go fishing early in the morning on the rocks in Vada, I often saw the float sink, I used to pull it up, and notice that the nylon thread had a clean cut near the hook.

I couldn't understand why, at first, I thought it was because of the bluefish, then I realized that it was because of the goldfish, the larger ones. Goldfish have sharp teeth and they can often cut threads that are thinner than 0.20.

3.
THE RIGHT ATTITUDE FOR FISHING

I remember once catching a rather big mullet. My fishing rod was very bent, so bent that I managed to attract the attention of the people on the beach. Some people had come right up next to me to watch the scene close-up and to see what kind of fish it was.

Instead of swimming frantically and strongly, the mullet started shaking its head trying get the hook out of its mouth.

It was pulling the fishing rod strongly. I managed to bring it almost to the shore. It was beautiful to see the silver reflection beneath the surface of the water.

The mullet continued shaking its head and pulling. It was a constant pull, until a stronger pull pushed the fishing rod back, loosening all the tension.

Just think, it had managed to break the 0.20 nylon thread. I can't describe the disappointment of those who were watching me, their comments were like:

"That mullet was beautiful, what a pity! You lost it. "

They stared at me, perhaps hoping to see disappointment on my face, or perhaps to hear some cursing or some kind of explanation.

They were very surprised when they heard me say in my calm tone of voice:

"I would have put it back into the water anyway, I managed to see it, it was exciting, so that's okay! "

They were not used to hearing a fisherman talk like that. I always threw the fish that I caught back into the water, and when people saw me do this, they were amazed. Fisherman usually take the fish they catch from the sea back home to eat. I went fishing almost every day and people started to recognize me, I was the one who threw the fish back into the sea, I often heard their comments. Mothers would say to their children:

"Have you seen that gentleman, he throws the fish back into the sea just like your father does in the river"

or other people would say:

"That's a sport fisherman practicing catch and release"

And others:

"Why do you throw it back in? Isn't it good? Why don't you give it to me?"

Sometimes I gave the fish to the grateful people who asked me for them but to the question they asked me

"Why do you throw them back?"

I would answer:

"After giving us so much enjoyment, the least we can do is to give them back their freedom."

As I think you may have understood, I am not a one of those fishermen who carry nets with them to put the fish in. I only bring the bare minimum equipment, this gives me some advantages. When I don't like the place where I'm fishing, I can move elsewhere in a moment.

I acquired the experience I now have after trying various fishing techniques in the river, thanks above all, to practice but also to the fishing courses I took in the past.

Among the various techniques, however, there is one in particular that has been very important for my growth, and it is also the one that made me understand the true message of fishing: fly fishing.

It made me understand that it is not the fish you catch, but how you catch it. It taught me respect for nature, for the river and for the fish.

Fishing is nothing but a cunning game between us and the fish, it is a continuous challenge, we try to do our best by using our skills and abilities, while fish use their survival instinct.

Sometimes the fish wins, sometimes we do, but we must remember to respect the fish, because it is thanks to the fish itself that we sometimes experience beautiful and unforgettable emotions. After giving us enjoyment, to give it back to nature, whether its the sea or the river, is a sign of respect for nature and for the fish itself.

4. THE RIGHT TECHNIQUE

Now I want to talk about fishing with the Bolognese rod. After throwing the line, keep it tight by watching the float and pull back very slowly, if you look carefully you will see the ball of bread followed by the fish that will then attack it.

Often, even many times, you can catch fish this way, it stays on the hook during the very slow recovery, with this technique we can especially catch leerfish and also saddled breams.

I never leave more than 70 cms from the float to the hook, a maximum of 1 mt, no more.

When surface fishing, we can also use two hooks. After the float we have to leave a loose piece of line of aprox 70 cm which we will tie to a swivel.

We will divide the line in 2 parts, one 30cm long and the other 45cm.

The two lines that hang from the swivel should never be the same length as thay would prevent the biting.

To your surprise, sometimes you will catch 2 fish together. On my YouTube channel "Lelio" you can find some videos showing you this.

This is the throwing technique:

- Throw

- Pull back slowly to keep the line tight

- Get ready to observe the school of fish that will rush towards the bait

Initially the float will move slightly and then sink or it will float on the surface. This is the right time to grasp.

To better understand when it is the right time to pull, try some test launches without trying to catch the fish.

Just watch the float sink, you will see that once it has sunk, it will come back up and it will stay still because the bread has already been eaten.

Try it, this will help you improve the timing of your grasp.

After trying a few times and once you have honed the sense of the grasp, put the bread on the hook again and then be prepared to pull immediately as soon as you see that small movement the float makes.

You will find that not all fish bite in the same way. For example, mullets will give you a good deal of trouble in understanding when they are eating. If you have never fished for mullets, the first few times, the float will look like it is always still.

But if you begin to observe more carefully, you will find that at the beginning of the bite, the float releases small vibrations and you will notice small circles in the water, that move away from the float.

The right moment to pull is during the first two or three of these circles. A very important thing. Remember to throw bait at the beginning. That's the first thing to do as soon as you arrive at the fishing spot.

Do it at regular intervals by throwing more bread into the sea. It won't be long before the mullets arrive. My equipment for mullet fishing is as follows.

I almost always use a 4 mt Bolognese rod, which for me is ideal, the nylon is 0.20, I use a small egg sinker for the float, secured below a small swivel, then 2 long lines, one 30 cm long and the other 45 cm long.

This time we will use dry bread. The soft inside of the bread such as baguettes or white sliced bread is fine.

Put the hook in the bread twice and press it partially on the pallet, to avoid losing it during the launch.

Keep the thread slightly tight and observe when the fish are eating, you will see the mullets around the float competing for the bait, right around the small pieces of bread; they will make a slight lapping of the small splashes that will indicate that this is the right time to pull.

Mullets are so greedy for bread that their feed will only take a few seconds.

When fishing for mullet it is always best to pull in advance. Mullets eat everything on the hooks without you even having the time to see the float move.

It is a type of fishing that you need to practice visually and you need to carefully calculate the right time to pull.

If the wind rises or the sea starts to get rough, it is advisable to stop due to the lack of the visibility of the float.

5. WHICH TYPE OF BREAD IS SUITABLE FOR FISHING

If we use fresh bread, that is, freshly baked bread, then almost all types of bread are ok, although olive oil bread rolls or classic baguettes are preferable. To prepare the bread bait, just open the bread, remove a small portion with your fingers, being careful not to press it, then insert the hook into the bread and try to hide it well.

Then press the whole thing with your fingers on the palette, so that it doesn't fall off during the launch.

French bread

The bread which is mostly used in sport fishing is the one you can buy from the hunting and fishing shops, is has a plait shape and is sold in a greaseproof paper packet.

It is very simple to prepare. Soak it for a few minutes, then put it into a cotton cloth to wring it out and then press it with your hands.

If you like, from time to time, you can remove small strips and place them on the hook at one end, then twist them twice around the hook and finally place it back on the hook again, leaving the opposite end loose.

Dough

The classic do-it-yourself dough is good. The bread dough is very simple to prepare, put some pieces of bread or bread rolls in a container with water, when the bread has absorbed the water, remove it from the container and squeeze it with your hands, removing as much water as possible.

Then take a cotton rag (I use an old kitchen tea-towel) and put the bread into it, it needs to be crushed by hand and then we add white flour, until it becomes a soft dough so that it does not stick to your hands.

To make it more compact you can also add breadcrumbs. Work on the dough by kneading it continuously with your hands, just like when you prepare pizza dough, only that it must be softer, it must be very soft. The secret of the dough is its softness, the softer it is, the more the fish will bite.

Obviously, you can put the bread either on the hook or on the small anchor.

Some people also add aromas to the mixture such as grated cheese or anchovy paste or other strong flavors. I think bread is enough, once its in the water the bread will release a very fragrant and attractive smell.

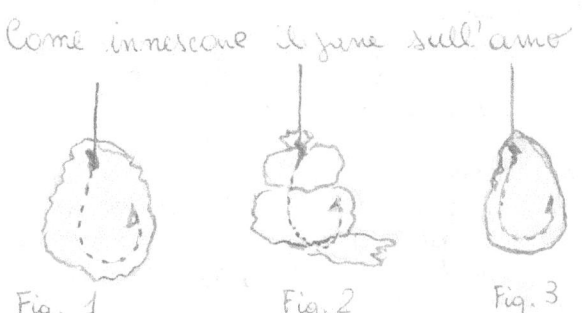

Come innescare il pane sull'amo

Fig. 1   Fig. 2   Fig. 3

Fig 1 = Fiocco di mollica di pane
Si infila l'amo dentro la mollica, nascondendolo bene. Si pressa con le punte delle dita sulla paletta.

Fig 2 = Fiocco di pane francese
Va bagnato prima dell'uso e strizzarlo bene. Si stacca un filo cuore, e si penetra con l'amo da una estremità, poi lo si gira 2 volte intorno all'amo, poi si penetra ancora una volta. Deve svolazzare con l'estremità opposta.

Fig 3 = Il pastone o pastella
Si mette a bagno il pane, lo strizziamo bene, possiamo aggiungere pane grattato, per dargli la giusta consistenza. Prendere una quantità sufficiente da coprire l'amo, modellarla a forma di una piccola pera. Possiamo pescare sia con l'amo o ancorina.

How to place the bread on the hook

Pic 1 = Bread dough
Insert the hook in the dough, making sure to hide it properly.
Press it properly with your fingers

Pic 2 = French bread dough
Soak and rinse properly before use. Take a strip and place it on the hook at one end, twist it around the hook twice, hook it on again and leave the opposite end loose.

Pic 3 = Homemade dough
Soak the bread, wring it out, it is possible to add bread crumbs to give it the right consistancy. Take a piece that is sufficient to hide the hook, mould it into a small pear shape. Fish either with the hook or with the small anchor.

White sliced sandwich bread

White sliced bread is my favorite, as it is a type of bread that immediately absorbs water, just soak it quickly, then squeeze it properly with your hands and then place it on a cotton cloth, this cloth has a dual function, it will remove the moisture left and it will prevent the sun from drying it out.

Place the small pear shape of bread on the hook.

6.
AVOID UNNECESSARY EQUIPMENT

With this chapter I would like to give you a specific message. Try not to make the mistake of filling yourself up with unnecessary equipment.

When I was a boy, I only had a fishing rod, it was more suitable for the river than for the sea. I had very few hooks and floats that were not appropriate for the sea.

I always fished with this little equipment, but by making a necessity a virtue, I had developed an excellent knowledge of my rod, I practised so much that me and my rod were one and the same thing and I acquired that sixth sense that allowed me to make up for all those shortcomings that my equipment had.

Later on, however, when I happened to enter a hunting and fishing shop, I was fascinated by all the types of rods they had. They were so beautiful! New and in various sizes and colours. I looked at all those floats that had such inviting shapes and colours, they seemed to be waiting only for me.

I heard a small voice coming from the floats, and each of them seemed to say to me:

Buy me! Buy me! "

I thought:

"If only I had those fishing rods, if only I had those floats, who knows how many fish I would catch"

And since then every time I went into a hunting and fishing shop, I always purchased. I always bought something, even though it would hardly be useful for my type of fishing, but I just couldn't resist.

Therefore, I found myself having so much equipment that even today I still haven't used it all. Oscar Wilde used to say:

"I can resist anything except temptations!"

I'm certainly not better than Oscar Wilde and so...

7. THE IMPORTANT THINGS TO KNOW

Tides

A fundamental piece of advice. Before going fishing, it is advisable to observe the sea the day before.

You have to check the time the tide goes out, this is called low tide. It is not advisable to fish at this time.

During this time, the fish will be distant from the shore, because the current will have dragged out everything that the fish feed on with it.

Instead, observe when the tide comes back in, that is when you see the uncovered rocks covered by the water again, that is the right time to fish.

This movement is called the high tide.

The fishing environment: natural and artificial reefs

All the natural and artificial reefs that we find at sea are excellent for fishing.

They are full of small caves, ravines (that are coves where fish hide) where fish continually roam searching for food.

If you look at them closely, they are full of vegetation, the more seaweed there is on the rocks under water, the better, you will also see limpets, sea urchins, crabs, these are clues that indicate that the place is perfect.

You should always fish where the water is deeper near the rocks, always remember that the first thing to do when you arrive in a place is to throw bait in the range of your fishing rod.

But don't only do it at the beginning, continue at regular intervals throughout the duration of your fishing session.

In this scenario you will fish sea breams, goldlines which are the classic deepwater fish, but also those fish that live in the mid-deep waters or even surface fish such as mullets, saddled breams and leerfish.

Fig 1: *Both natural and artificial reefs are paradise for fishermen*

Fig 2: *Degrading rocky coastline with rocks emerging from under the water A great place for sea breams and saddled breams.*

Fig 3: *Reef ocean floor with underwater meadows, excellent for sea breams and mullets*

Fig 4: *A varied ocean floor, good for all types of fish*

The fishing environment: river mouths

River outlets, as well as channels that flow into the sea, are one of the best places for fishing. The river floors are almost always sandy, medium-shallow in depth but populated enough by different species of fish.

Many different mullets can be found, that swim up the rivers for several kilometers, given their ability to adapt to fresh waters.

At the beginning of the outlet you will also find leerfish that constantly roam in search of food.

Always fish in the deepest point and where the current is calmer, this will allow you to have a slower pace (by slower pace I mean where you are fishing there is little current, therefore it allows you to observe the float properly) allowing the bait to touch the bottom where it will be chased and attacked by the fish that are in the area at that moment.

8. FISH MEASUREMENTS

In order to avoid possible fines by the authorities, it is best to know the minimum measurements of the fish. The size is calculated from the mouth to the extreme part of the closed caudal fin. Here below are the minimum fish sizes in Italy.

COMMON NAME	SCIENTIFIC NAME	MIN. MEASURES
Anchovy	Engraulis encrasicolus	9 cm.
Garfish	Belone belone	25 cm.
Eel	Anguilla anguilla	28 cm.
Bogue	Boops boops	7 cm.
Mullet	Mugil cephalus	20 cm.
Brown meagre	Sciaena umbra	20 cm.
Dentex	Dentex dentex	30 cm.
Conger eel	Conger conger	50 cm.
Amia leerfish	Lichia amia	60 cm.
Star leerfish	Trachinotus Ovatus	7 cm.
Barracuda	Sphyraena sphyraena	30 cm.
Striped seabream	Lithognathus mormyrus	15 cm.

Moray	Muraena helena	60 cm.
Saddled bream	Oblada melanura	7 cm.
Corb	Umbrina cirrosa	25 cm.
Gilthead bream	Sparus aurata	20 cm.
Goldline	Sarpa salpa	07 cm.
Two-banded seabream	Diplodus vulgaris	18 cm.
Sharpsnout seabream	Diplodus puntazzo	18 cm.
Zebra seabream	Diplodus sargus	23 cm.
Mackerel	Scomber scombrus	18 cm.
Annular seabream	Diplodus anularis	12 cm.
Bass	Dicentrarchus labrax	25 cm.
Scad	Trachurus trachurus	12 cm.
Black seabream	Spondyliosoma cantharus	7 cm.
Green Wrasse	Labrus viridis	7 cm.

9. THE MAIN TYPE OF FISH THAT WILL BITE BREAD

The Bogue

BOGA
(Boops boops)

The bogue belongs to the Sparida families. Its body is tapered, it has a rather small mouth, but it has very sharp teeth that can often cut very thin nylon thread. Its body reflects colours ranging from yellow to light green. It doesn't grow very large, it rarely reaches 30 cms. The sides and the stomach of the fish are silver.

This fish has very large eyes. The translation of the scientific name "Boops boops" is the "eye of the ox". The best season for fishing this type of fish is summer, but autumn is also good, and almost all hours of the day are ok. You can find it near both natural and artificial reefs, in mixed territories, where there is sand, rocks and the seagrass of the posidonia ocean beds.

It is a very easy fish to catch. When it is close to the rocks it is preferable to use a fixed fishing rod, it is faster to catch. Bogues move in large schools and you can catch many of them in a short time. Of course, the shorter and lighter the fishing rod, the less tired your arm will get.

I recommend a 0.18 nylon thread, a very small ball shaped float and to tie an 18 sized hook with a long stem and a tiny ball of pear-shaped bread, a meter from the float The sinkers must be grouped at about 10 or 15cms from the hook. One split sinker will be sufficient. Always remember to chum thoroughly with bread before and during fishing.

The Mullet

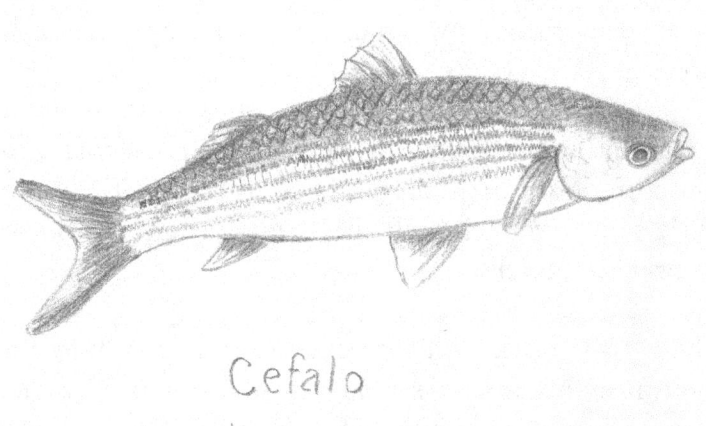

Cefalo
(Mugil cephalus)

Its Latin name is Mugil Cephalus, it is also called the mullet and belongs to the elongated fish group. It is a very elegant fish, its body is long, sturdy and strong and flattens towards the tail.

Its overall color is silver, which is darker on the back and lighter at the sides and on the stomach. This fish is a tireless swimmer, its resistance, once-hooked, is impressive.

It can be caught all year long even if the best seasons for it are spring, summer and autumn. Any time of the day is good.

It is found in both salt and fresh water, in harbors, near the cliffs, both artificial and natural, and also in the outlets of rivers, in which it enters and swims for several kilometers.

These fish move in large schools, you can often find them near organic waste dumps, and this is why their meat sometimes has an unpleasant taste. You can catch them with the fixed or even with the Bolognese fishing rod.

Catching Mullets with a fixed fishing rod

It is ideal to use a fixed fishing rod possibly made of carbon with a point of action from 5 to 6.50 mts.

I suggest a nylon thread of 0.16, 40 cm shorter than the fishing rod. The float must have a very tapered shape and must go from 0.5 to 1.5 gms maximum.

At the end tie a swivel where you can tie another two ends using an 0.12 nylon thread. One thread must be 30 cm long and the other 60 cm.

The size of the long and thin stem hooks will vary from 16 to 10. It is preferable to group the weight on top of the swivel with split 0.12 lead pellets.

It is preferable to use French bread as bait, soaked and squeezed very well before using, tear a piece off, then penetrate the hook at one end, then twist it twice around the hook and penetrate the hook again to leave the appropriate end loose.

Before starting to fish chum in the area by throwing balls of bread the size of an orange which has been previously soaked and properly squeezed, in the water.

Do this even while fishing at regular intervals, keep throwing handfuls of bread into the water.

Take a small bucket with you to prepare the bread, and of course, also take a lot of bread with you. Remember to immediately pull with determination as soon as you see the rod of the float sink. The mullets bite only lasts a few seconds therefore it is better to anticipate it rather than to be late.

If the school of mullets is on the surface, then fishing shallow waters, no more than one meter deep, viceversa measure the bottom of the water with a probe and keep the bait about 10 cm from the bottom.

Mullets with the Bolognese rod

When mullets are far from the shore it is better to fish with the Bolognese rod. If you are fishing from low cliffs a 4 mt rod will be fine.

However, if you are fishing from high cliffs, you could have to use even a 7 mt rod.

When the water is calm and there is no wind, I use the English 4 + 1 float with about a 70 cm loose end, a small anchor size 14 and white sliced sandwich bread previously soaked and properly squeezed with a cotton cloth.

In this case, we use the small anchor hook, because when throwing further you risk losing the bait, but with the anchor hook that holds the bread properly you will throw the line with greater security.

After throwing do not keep the bait still, but pull it in very slowly, keeping the fishing line tight, you will see the float and the ball of bread almost afloat.

When you see the school of mullets stop, the mullets will attack the bread greedily, sinking the float or moving it to the side.

Remember to pull immediately with determination.

When the water begins to move it is preferable to use the classic egg-shaped float with a 2 to 6 gm sinker.

If the sea is slightly rough, it is preferable to use a shorter loose end, 30cm will be enough, with a small anchor, soaked white bread shaped into a small pear-shaped ball.

After throwing, pull in very slowly, again this time when you see the mullets arrive, stop and wait.

When you see some splashing or water moving around the float, it means that they are greedily eating the bait.

It is best to pull immediately, otherwise the bread will be finished in an instance. The mullet will not always stay attached, this is part of the game.

Remember mullets very rarely swallow the bait, they suck it with their lips, sometimes they slither over it to flake it and then suck it, that's why mullets rarely sink the float, it's up to us to learn to choose the right moment to catch them.

Mullet

Saddled bream

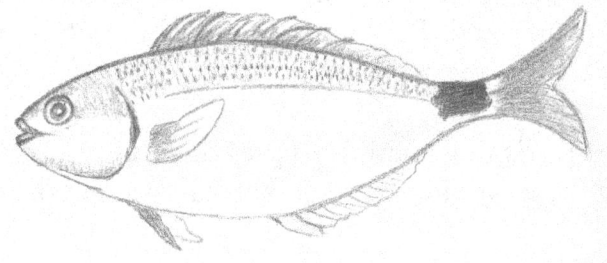

Occhiata

(Oblada melanura)

Its Latin name is Oblada Melanura and it belongs to the order of the elongated fish-shaped.

Its body is oval, it is flattened on the sides and it is silver in colour. At the end of its body, near its tail, it has a dark mark that together with its large eyes, it has earned the name "occhiata" in Italian which means "gaze".

In spring mullets approach the shore in big schools. They love the rocky coasts that are both deep and shallow. They also prefer rocky seabeds, with algae mixed with sand. They don't get very big and can reach 30 cms at the most.

The ideal fishing conditions are when the sea is rough, when the waves hit the rocks and cause a trail of surf.

A rigid fixed rod long enough to get past the surf is ideal. It is preferable to use the line without the float, with a small anchor-hook size 16 or 14 with bread.

Throw the line beyond the surf letting the bait sink naturally. Let it hang while you move it very slowly from one side to the other until you find the fish.

Mullets bite immediately, but you must be quick in pulling, because their capture can scare the rest of the fish who run away. Of course, the end must be strong enough, a 0.18 or a 0.20 is fine.

Fishing with the Bolognese rod is also good with a reel loaded with 0,18 weight. For the float we will use the classic egg or ball shaped sinker if the water is very rough. The weight should be from 3 to 8 grams.

For the end, I recommend using about 1 meter of 0.16 fluorcarbon with a 14 sized anchor-hook on which you can place some bread.

The best time for fishing is in autumn, but you can get a good catch even in spring and in summer.

Saddled bream

Goldline

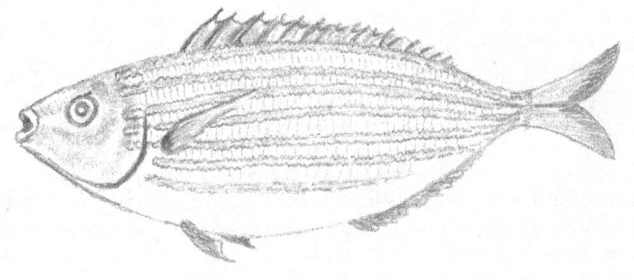

Salpa

(Boops salpa)

Goldlines (Sarpa salpa or Boops salpa) belong to the Sparidae family. It is a very combative and fun fish.

It is very commonly found in the Mediterranean, near the rocky stretches, low reefs and mixed seabeds, as long as there is seaweed, its favorite food.

Observe the cliffs calmly, the ones with green tufts of seaweed that move with the current, rest assured that the goldlines will be there.

To fish goldlines in the right way you will need powerful fishing rods, whether they are fixed rods or the Bolognese rods.

Goldlines have very sharp pointed teeth, so I suggest you never use an end that is under 0.20.

Since we are fishing near the rocks, I prefer a float that weighs 1 gram and a loose end of about 120 or 150cms.

The hook must be long-stemmed and of a good size, from 14 up to 8.

As bait, classic bread is fine or white sliced bread soaked and properly squeezed, the amount must be quite substantial.

Retrieving goldlines is quite challenging, you must keep them as far as possible from the rocks, as they can slip into cracks or any other obstacle making the line rub against them and causing it to break.

They are a lot of fun, they will pull your line far and wide and will not give up very easily. Once they are tired and exhausted, I recommend using the landing net.
If you decide to cook this fish, I suggest you remove the insides and rinse repeatedly in the sea before taking it home.

The goldlines main food supply is seaweed so in order to avoid this fermenting, which would give the meat an unpleasant and strong taste, it is best to take this precaution.

Pompano

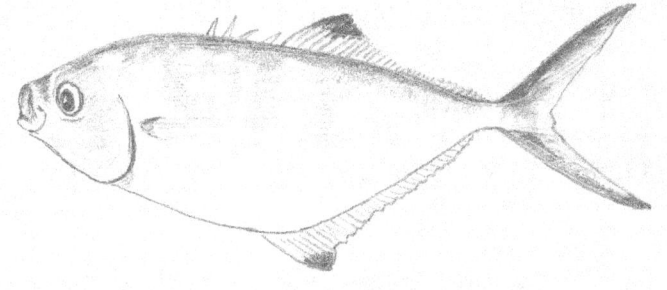

Leccia stella
(Trachinotus glaucus)

Pompano (Trachinotus Ovatus or Trachinotus Glaucus) is part of the Carangidae family. It has an oval shaped body, it is compressed at the sides with a small mouth and rather large eyes compared to its body.

The anal fins and the first dorsal are arranged symmetrically and opposite each other.

Its tail is narrow and long and very V shaped. Its body is a very pearly white color, it has darker spots on the sides while the tips of the fins are black.

It hardly reaches 50 cm in length and it can weight up to 2 kgs. It is found throughout the Mediterranean Sea and in the Eastern Atlantic Ocean.

It is very common near the coasts and also at the outlets of rivers. It approaches our shores during the months of June, July, August and September.

A bait that it can't resist is sliced white bread, just wet (not soaked) and immediately wrung with a cloth.

Once in the water it leaves a trail of smell which is irresistible, and in fact it attacks the bread quite violently.

I suggest to use the Bolognese rod, with a weighted float, that is ball shaped or with a classic egg shape, the weight of the float will depend on the fish, if they are close 3 gms is fine, if they are further away even 6 or 8 grams.

If you fish near the shore, about a 1mt thread or so is enough, I put a swivel on the end of it, on which I tie another 2 loose ends, one of 30cm and one of 45 cm with hooks ranging from size 14 to 10 on which I place a ball of pear-shaped bread.

The bite of a Pompano is very determined, it is not uncommon, considering that you are fishing with two hooks, to catch two of them together.

As mentioned earlier, on my You Tube channel, you can find some videos showing this.

If the school of Pompano is further away, you should increase the weight of the float, decrease the thread, that must be about 70 cms or so, but this time you will use a small anchor size 12 or 14 on the end, of course always place bread on it but make sure it is a more abundant portion this time.

For a longer throw the small sinker is ideal because it holds the bread better and you will avoid losing it.

When you fish away from the shore in order to chum, throw in the bait three or four times freely, this way the bread will stay there and will attract the fish.

The next time, after launching, pull in very slowly, as soon as you see the school of fish arrive, stop pulling and get ready as the float will start moving very quickly, then pull immediately!

Pompano are good fighters, you will have fun bringing them to shore. Its meat is well appreciated in the kitchen.

Sargo (White Seabream)

SARAGO

Its Latin name is Diplodus Sargus, it's part of the elongated fish-shape order and belongs to the Sparidae family. Its body has an elliptical oval shape, and is laterally compressed.

It has a protruding mouth, big eyes, and is silver and white on the stomach. It is found throughout the Mediterranean Sea, in the Tyrrhenian Sea and in all those areas that have mixed ocean floors, full of molluscs.

You can find it in the rocky shores, inside the harbors, in natural and artificial reefs, in these underwater areas where micro-organisms that give life to all the small algae and tufts of grass develop.

There are different types of Sea breams; Sheepshead bream, Zebra seabream, white bream and two-banded bream. When the sea starts to move, it is the best time to fish for sea bream.

A 6 to 8 mt bolognese rod is ideal, combined with a 2500 reel with a good 0.18.

I recommend a round-shaped float, adjusted so that the bait floats about 20 cm from the bottom and the use of a small anchor size 12, because it holds the bread better.

I prefer white sliced bread because it is easy to prepare.

Chum your fishing area properly, when the fish will see our good bait, they will violently and decisively attack it, showing us spectacular bites.

It's defense is very powerful, you have to pull it in decicively, because if it manages to get into a small hiding space, you can say goodbye to it immediately.

Sargo

Other fish occasionally caught with bread

Those that I have just listed are the classic fish that you can catch with bread, but there are many others to catch while fishing with bread.

For example, gilthead breams. If caught at the shore, they do not tend to be very big, they are the classic "small sea beams", however you can enjoy catching them even with bread.

Sometimes in the evening when the sun sets, I have occasionally caught some rockfish. If it happens to you, be very careful because their bites are very painful, I know from experience.

Even painted combers like bread, as soon as they stay attached on the hook, they have a very strong defense, but after a few moments they come up very easily.

You should know that when the sea is calm, schools of silversides and sardines arrive.

Using a 4.5mt fixed rod and using a light armor, like a 0.10 nylon thread and a hook size 18, you can have a lot of fun and you can take a big amount home.

For thoose who love fryed fish, this is the ideal type of fish. Remember, of course, to chum often.

Even the ornate wrasse can be caught with bread.

Meditarrenan rainbow wrasse (Thalassoma pavo)

See how many different fish you can catch with bread? Isn't this bait fantastic? It's very easy to prepare, it's clean, we always have it on hand, you do not have to go the hunting and fishing shop to buy worms of any sort or any other live baits.

Threrefore you do not have to worry about keeping the bait in the fridge to make it last either, or cool in the garage.

Do you know how many people have left a bag of maggots in the garage, that managed to escape and ended up everywhere?

After a while, you get a lot of flies, there are people who have opened their garage to find hundreds of flies flying out. In these moments you have to hope that your wife doesn't need to go to into the garage, otherwise...

Jokes aside, this can also happen, but this problem does not exist with bread!

Conclusion

Lastly, I left the most important thing above everything else, which is what really makes the difference. I want you to pay attention to this. Have you ever wondered why fish attack artificial bait in spinning fishing?

For as similar as it can be, artificial bait is always an inanimate body, whether it is made of metal or silicone, it will never be edible, if it was lying still on the bottom it would only cause curiosity.

It is the movement that makes an inanimate body come to life, it is the movement that triggers the attack in the fish. We do not know if it's beacuse of hunger, curiosity, or territorial defense, but this is what happens.

Be aware that with bread you have twice the chance of catching a fish. We all know that fish bite bread even when it stays still, but have you ever tried to move it as well?

To your surprise, try this technique of mine. After throwing the line, hold it tight, pull in very slowly, alternate short pauses with a slow recovery. So, while you pull back slowly, stop only when you see the fish coming and wait for them to bite. If not, throw again.

You must imagine that our mouthful of bread is a small cuttlefish that is slowly swimming, the white color and the movement will attract the fish that will want to see what it is.

Remember that something that moves is more visible than something that stays still.

This simple logic has always made me catch a lot of fish, try again and again until you get the same results as I have. That said, I can now leave wishing you the very best of luck.

LELIO ZELONI

SIMPLE FISHING WITH BREAD

The Secret? Experience!

YouTube: Lelio Pesca
Facebook: Lelio Pesca
Instagram: Lelio Pesca

leliopesca.com
fishingwithbread.com
pescareconilpane.com
pescaconpan.com

www.ingramcontent.com/pod-product-compliance
Lightning Source LLC
Chambersburg PA
CBHW072206100526
44589CB00015B/2394